SPACE

The Solar System

Robin Birch

An Imprint of Chelsea House Publishers
A Haights Cross Communications Company
Philadelphia

This edition first published in 2003 in the United States of America by Chelsea Clubhouse, a division of Chelsea House Publishers and a subsidiary of Haights Cross Communications.

All rights reserved. No part of this publication may be reproduced or transmitted in any form or by any means without the written permission of the publisher.

Chelsea Clubhouse
1974 Sproul Road, Suite 400
Broomall, PA 19008-0914

The Chelsea House world wide web address is www.chelseahouse.com

Library of Congress Cataloging-in-Publication Data

Birch, Robin.
 The solar system / by Robin Birch.
 p. cm. — (Space)
 Includes index.
 Summary: An introduction to our solar system, including information on the sun, planets, moons, comets, and asteroids.
 ISBN 0-7910-6969-9
 1. Solar system—Juvenile literature. [1. Solar system.] I. Title.
 QB501.3 .B57 2003
 523.2—dc21

2002000038

First published in 2001 by
MACMILLAN EDUCATION AUSTRALIA PTY LTD
627 Chapel Street, South Yarra, Australia, 3141

Copyright © Robin Birch 2001
Copyright in photographs © individual photographers as credited

Edited by Carmel Heron and Louisa Kost
Cover and text design by Anne Stanhope
Illustrations by Frey Micklethwait

Printed in China

Acknowledgements

Cover photograph: Stars in Milky Way galaxy, courtesy of Michael Toms, supplied by Astrovisuals.

Photographs courtesy of: Astrovisuals, p. 29; Digital Vision, p. 12 (bottom right); FPG International/Austral, p. 28; Getty Images, p. 27; NASA, pp. 12 (bottom left), 14 (top left and bottom right), 24; NASA, supplied by Astrovisuals, pp. 12, 13 (top), 14 (bottom left), 16, 18, 22, 25; National Optical Australian Observatory, supplied by Astrovisuals, p. 20; Photodisc, p. 26; Photo Essentials, pp. 14 (top right), 17; Photolibrary.com/Robin Smith, p. 8; Photolibrary.com/Science Photo Library, p. 19; Michael Toms, supplied by Astrovisuals, pp. 1, 6.

While every care has been taken to trace and acknowledge copyright the publisher tenders their apologies for any accidental infringement where copyright has proved untraceable.

Contents

4	What Is the Solar System?
6	Where Is the Solar System?
8	Earth and the Sun
10	Planets
16	Moons
20	Comets
22	Asteroids
24	Exploring the Solar System
26	Life in the Solar System
28	Watching the Solar System
30	Solar System Facts
31	Glossary
32	Index

What Is the Solar System?

The solar system is the Sun and everything that moves around it. Planets, comets, asteroids, and other objects in space **orbit** the Sun.

The solar system is very old. It is more than 4 billion years old. It formed from a huge cloud of gas and dust.

Earth and other objects in the solar system formed from gas and dust.

Where Is the Solar System?

Our solar system is in the Milky Way **galaxy**. The Milky Way contains millions of **stars** that are far from Earth. We can see the Milky Way. On a clear, dark night, it looks like a thin cloud across the sky.

Our solar system

The Milky Way galaxy has a **spiral** shape. Our solar system is found on one of the arms of the spiral. It is near the outside edge.

Earth and the Sun

We live in the solar system on the planet Earth. The Sun is the closest star to Earth. It is the center of our solar system. It gives us light and heat.

Earth orbits the Sun in a circular path. The time it takes for a planet to orbit the Sun once is called a year.

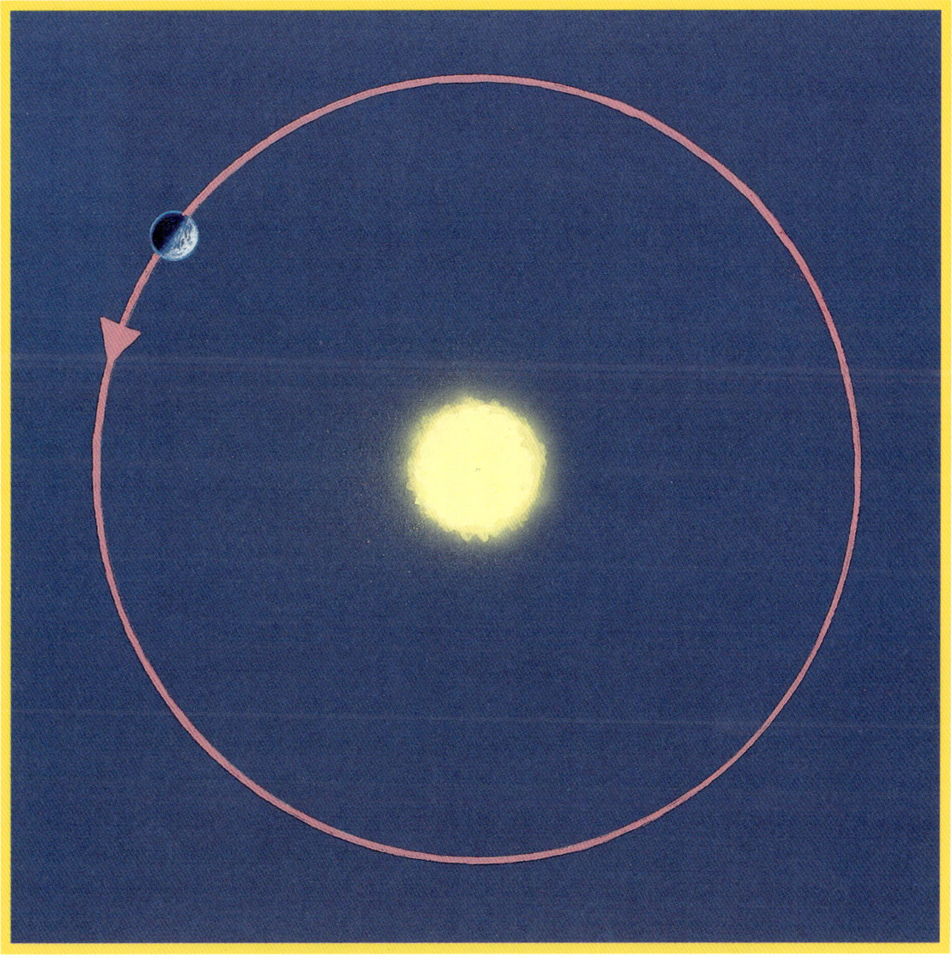

Planets

Planets are giant balls of rock or gas that move around a star. There are nine planets in our solar system. They all travel around the Sun.

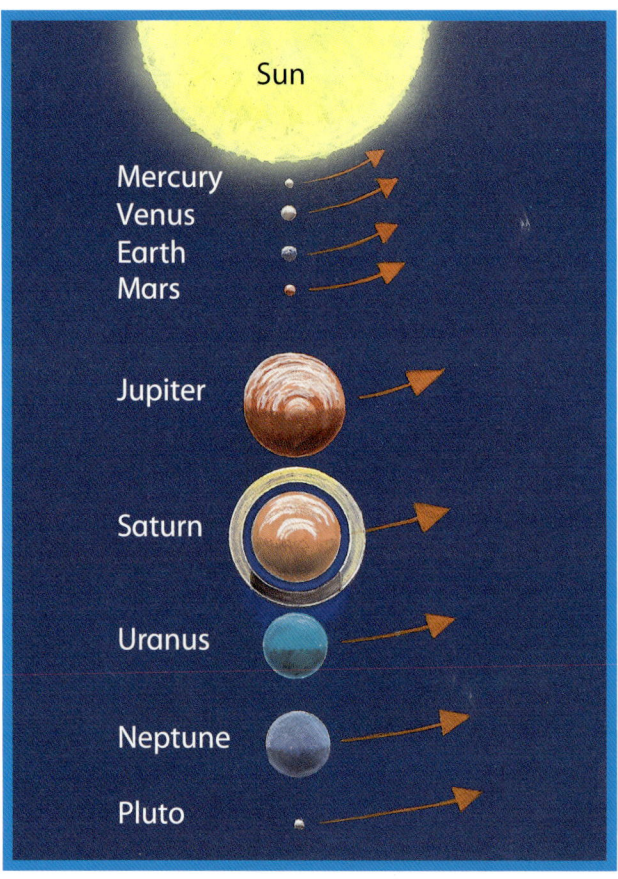

Each planet takes a different amount of time to orbit the Sun. We can compare other planets' years to Earth days or years. There are 365 days in one Earth year.

Planet Years		
1 Mercury year	=	88 Earth days
1 Venus year	=	225 Earth days
1 Earth year	=	365 Earth days
1 Mars year	=	about 2 Earth years
1 Jupiter year	=	about 12 Earth years
1 Saturn year	=	about 29 Earth years
1 Uranus year	=	about 84 Earth years
1 Neptune year	=	about 165 Earth years
1 Pluto year	=	about 249 Earth years

Rocky Planets

The closest planets to the Sun are made of rock. These planets are Mercury, Venus, Earth, and Mars. They are called the rocky planets.

Mercury

Venus

Earth

Mars

Pluto is the farthest planet from the Sun. It is also made of rock. All of the rocky planets are small planets.

Gas Giants

The four largest planets are made of gas. They are called the gas giants. Their names are Jupiter, Saturn, Uranus, and Neptune. There is no solid ground on these planets.

Jupiter

Saturn

Uranus

Neptune

The gas giants are very light for their size. Saturn could easily float in a swimming pool, if there was a pool large enough for it to fit!

Moons

Most of the planets have moons. A moon orbits around its planet. Earth has one moon made of rock. It takes about 27 days for the Moon to orbit Earth once.

Earth's Moon

Earth's moon is round like a ball. It is smaller than Earth. We mostly see it at night. It **reflects** light from the Sun. **Astronauts** have walked on Earth's moon.

Moon Shapes

Jupiter's moons and Saturn's moons are round, like Earth's moon. Jupiter has 16 moons, and Saturn has at least 30.

Saturn has at least 30 moons. This image shows six of them.

Other planets' moons have uneven shapes.
The two moons of Mars have uneven shapes.

Comets

Comets are made of ice, frozen gas, and dust. They also travel around the Sun. A comet heats up as it comes closer to the Sun. It glows more brightly, and a long tail appears. We sometimes see large comets from Earth.

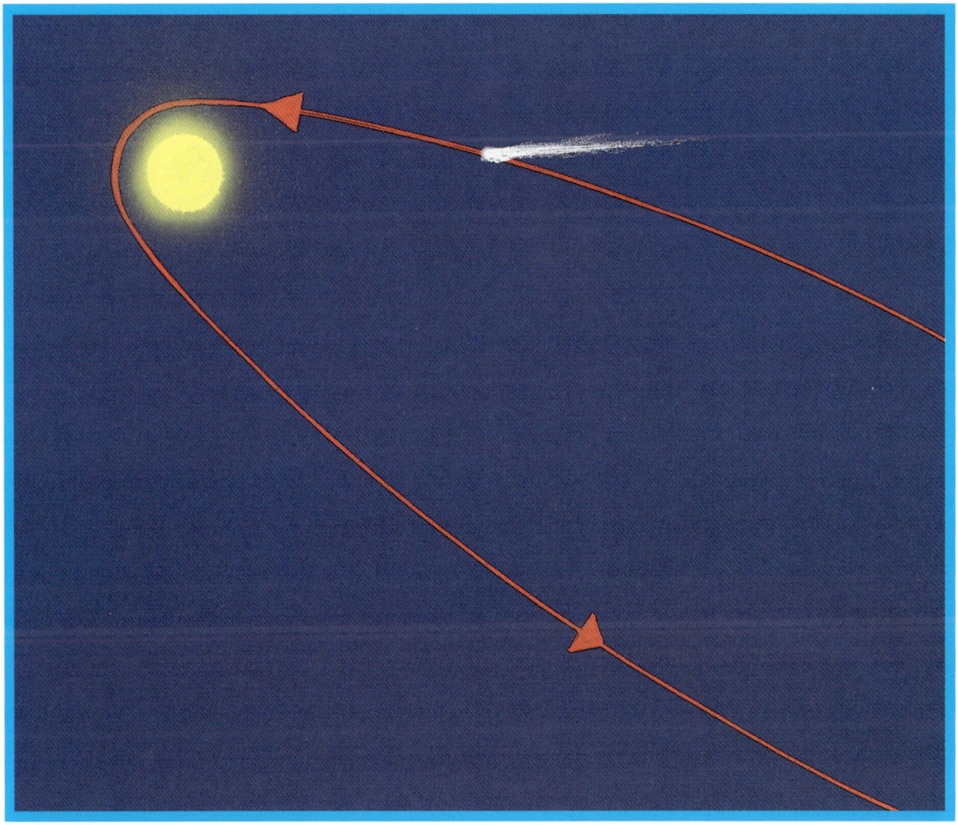

Comets start their journey a long way from the Sun. They come from places even farther out than Pluto. Comets circle close to the Sun, then they travel away again. Some comets keep coming back to the Sun. Others break apart.

Asteroids

Asteroids are pieces of rock that travel around the Sun. Some asteroids are round like balls. Other asteroids have uneven shapes. Asteroids are sometimes called **minor** planets.

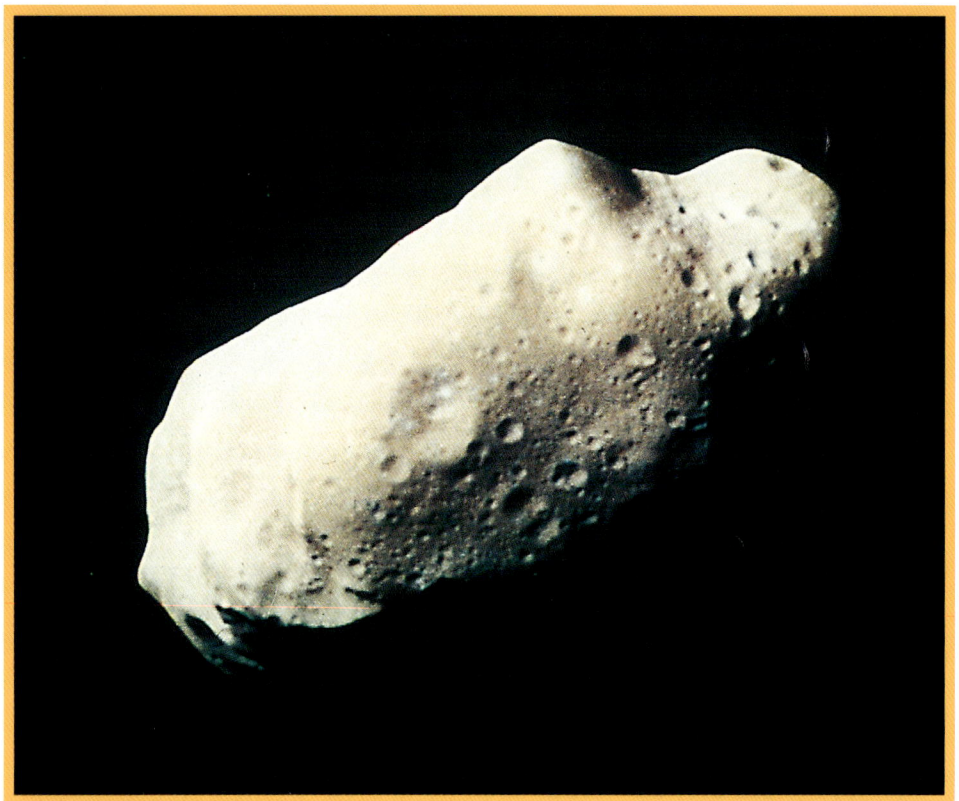

Most asteroids circle the Sun along a path called the asteroid belt. The asteroid belt is found between the orbits of Mars and Jupiter. There are millions of asteroids in space.

Exploring the Solar System

Space probes are space vehicles that do not carry people. They help scientists study the solar system. They use **radio waves** to send photographs and information back to Earth. The space probes *Voyager 1* and *Voyager 2* have taken many photographs of Jupiter, Saturn, Uranus, and Neptune.

The surface of Mars is rocky.

The space probes *Viking 1* and *Viking 2* landed on Mars. Scientists used them to take photographs and conduct experiments on the surface of Mars. The space probes sent radio waves back to Earth for nearly seven years.

Life in the Solar System

Earth is the only planet known to have life. Scientists continually search for signs of life on other planets.

A scientist studies rocks from space for signs of life.

Comets give us clues to whether there is other life in space.

Scientists have studied space matter from gas clouds and comets. Some of the matter is usually found only in living things. It shows that there could be other kinds of life in space.

Watching the Solar System

Parts of the solar system can be seen from Earth. The planets Mercury, Venus, Mars, Jupiter, and Saturn look like bright stars to us.

The planet Venus can be seen from Earth.

We sometimes see meteors at night. Meteors are small pieces of asteroids, rock, or dust that come toward Earth. We see a streak of light as a meteor burns up in our **atmosphere**. We sometimes call these meteors shooting stars.

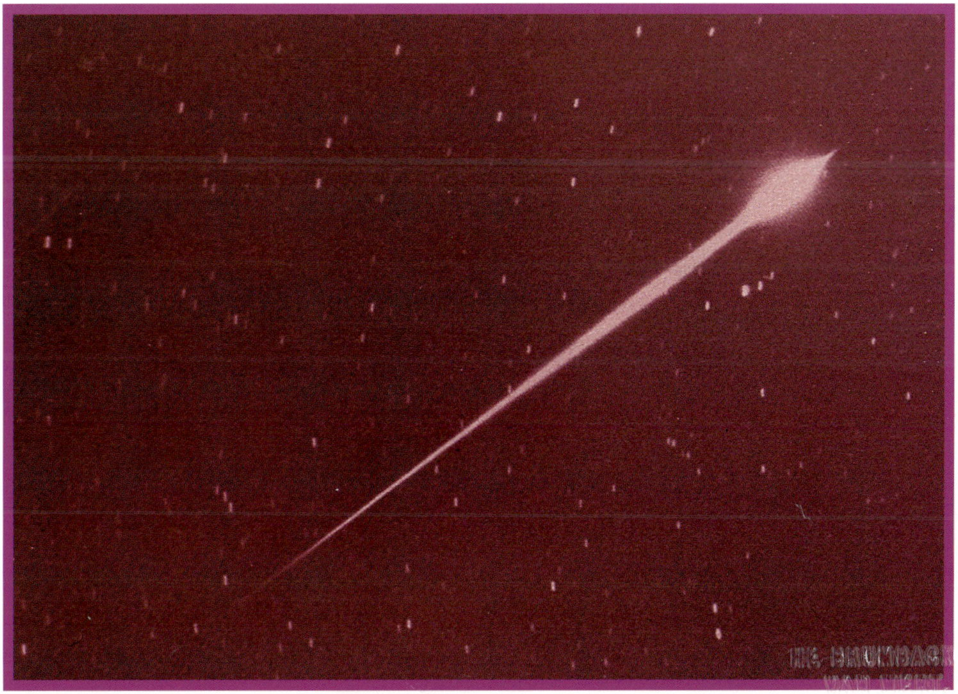

Some meteors look like shooting stars.

Solar System Facts

Name		Color	Made of	Number of Moons
Planets	Other Bodies			
	Sun	yellow	gas	0
	comets	white	ice	0
Mercury		gray	rock	0
Venus		gray and white	rock	0
Earth		blue and white	rock	1
Mars		red-brown	rock	2
	asteroids	gray	rock	0
Jupiter		orange, brown, white, red, yellow	gas	16
Saturn		gold	gas	30
Uranus		green-blue	gas	21
Neptune		blue	gas	8
Pluto		gray	rock	1

Glossary

astronaut — a person trained to travel and work in space

atmosphere — a mixture of gases that surround a planet

galaxy — a huge group of millions of stars

minor — small in size

orbit — to circle an object in space; also, the path that a planet or moon takes when circling another object.

radio waves — invisible rays that can carry information

reflect — to turn back; the Moon and the planets reflect light from the Sun.

spiral — a curved pattern that keeps winding around and around; a spring has a spiral shape.

star — a large, burning ball of gas in space; a star gives off light and heat.

Index

asteroid belt, 23

asteroids, 4, 22–23, 29, 30

astronauts, 17

atmosphere, 29

comets, 4, 20–21, 27, 30

Earth, 6, 8–9, 11, 12, 16–17, 18, 20, 24–25, 26, 28–29, 30

galaxy, 6–7

gas giants, 14–15

Jupiter, 11, 14, 18, 23, 24, 28, 30

life, 26–27

Mars, 11, 12, 19, 23, 25, 28, 30

Mercury, 11, 12, 28, 30

meteors, 29

Milky Way, 6–7

moons, 16–19

Neptune, 11, 14, 24, 30

planets, 4, 10–15, 16, 19, 26, 30

Pluto, 11, 13, 21, 30

radio waves, 24–25

rocky planets, 12–13

Saturn, 11, 14–15, 18, 24, 28, 30

scientists, 24–25, 26–27

shooting stars, 29

space probes, 24

stars, 6, 8, 10, 28

Sun, 4, 8–9, 10–13, 17, 20–21, 22–23, 30

Uranus, 11, 14, 24, 30

Venus, 11, 12, 28, 30

year, 9, 11